PRAISE FOR *WHOLE NIGHT THROUGH*

"I'm in awe of L.I. Henley's book-length narrative / persona-poem-sequence / novel-in-lyrics / poem-for-voices / dream-screenplay—we can invent a genre-label later, but the point is: *Whole Night Through* is a compelling, enticing read from first to last, a lyric-dramatic achievement by a truly visionary American poet. Like the best of her generation, L.I. Henley's language is fast and her imagery dense, but her ear is always out for the fierce silences of her characters' fears and desires. And she has heart—every poem-monologue here, no matter how violent, shows deep compassion for the men and women who wander through her desert landscape, confused but in possession of a fierce grace. I hope this book gets Henley the wide readership she deserves. The 21st century needs a vision like hers."

—James Cushing, San Luis Obispo Poet Laureate

WHAT BOOKS PRESS

AN IMPRINT OF

THE GLASS TABLE

COLLECTIVE

LOS ANGELES

ALSO BY L.I. HENLEY

Desert with a Cabin View
The Finding
These Friends These Rooms
Starshine Road

WHOLE NIGHT THROUGH

L.I. HENLEY

Copyright © 2019 by L.I. Henley. All rights reserved. Published in the United States by What Books Press, the imprint of the Glass Table Collective, Los Angeles.

Publisher's Cataloging-In-Publication Data
Names: Henley, L. I., 1984- author.
Title: Whole night through / L.I. Henley.
Description: Los Angeles : What Books Press, [2019]
Identifiers: ISBN 9781532341472
Subjects: LCSH: Couples--Mojave Desert--Poetry. | Country life--Mojave Desert--Poetry. | Homicide--Mojave Desert--Poetry. | Military bases--Mojave Desert--Poetry. | LCGFT: Poetry.
Classification: LCC PS3608.E553 W46 2019 | DDC 811/.6--dc23

Cover art: Gronk, *untitled*, watercolor and ink, 2018
Book design by Ash Good, www.ashgood.design

What Books Press
363 South Topanga Canyon Boulevard
Topanga, CA 90290

WHATBOOKSPRESS.COM

WHOLE NIGHT THROUGH

for Jonathan

CONTENTS

SECTION I

I can smoke a cigarette	3
Prom night in Branford	4
I didn't want her	5
Infinity stretches out between us	6
Heart at rest	7
Blue kettle knocking	8
There used to be	9
A fly landed on her shoulder	11
At the concert, lighters waved like	12
Ella's first horse, Red, kicked me hard	13
They both wore white as if it was their own private wedding	14
Night played taps with our spines	15
Will you go with me if I go?	16
Momma	17

SECTION II

When I see rabbits, I see him	21
When the sunflowers are quiet	22
The oaks of Branford, Florida	23
My head under his boot, my teeth	24
I didn't do it but I helped them	25
How do you count backwards	26
When you cry like that, all strung out	27

I like seeing people's faces through windshields	29
War games take me away for weeks	30
She was dancing like something that twists	31
First time I was alone with Michael	32
Michael buys me bracelets that I can't wear home	34
The painted quarter horse	35
The auburn Gelding	37
It's true I seen them kissing	38
Michael wants me like a road	39
Back in Louisiana, I knew a girl who hooked it	40
Born early, the blue hour between	42
My dreams unfurl, thousand-petal heads	43
I jump from the platform, a deep	44
She	45
Now I've failed and the failure tastes	46

SECTION III

Here is what I know about Jake	51
Sensitive	52
Jake imagined a string of pearls	53
Jake came to live with us	54
Jake grew a whole inch taller	55
Her impatience burns her	56
She wanted to wear her prom dress	57

Sometimes people hide in plain sight	58
My father's veterinarian office	59
Dance night in the community center	60
Say my name into a canyon	63
My mother is six months dead	64
She wants to know my plans	66
All day I've had the feeling that I don't belong	68
At the Break-n-Run Billiards	70
With the moving truck carried away by a brown cloud	73
People don't know this, but I married Ella and Jake	75

SECTION IV

I come to the pool by myself	79
An hour late. I stare at Michael's apartment door	80
A dove has made a nest under the concrete	81
Dear Jake	82
No coyote stops me in the road	83
My baby I love more than my husband	84
In the saloon, a man recognizes me	85
I drink a whiskey sour, but burned brisket	86
At the carnival, I see Michael	87
Michael wasn't at the meeting place—fooled again	88
Today I slept for hours on the speckled face	89
I could go back to the apartment	91
If I go home to Helena	92

In the absence of my other	93
If I name each place the meeting place	94
A nineteen-hour flight, concussed	95
I waited at the terminal	96
Every road is a gamble	97
My wife asks me about our neighbor	107
I've come to a wall where the phone	108
The walls pop and shift, expand—moan	109
My neighbor came home	110
When the call comes	112
The white doctor gave me white pills	114
After I tossed my last twenty	117
When I was a kid they wouldn't leave	119
At the Wal-Mart in Forty-Nine Palms	120
Lisa's been gone for a week	121
Gin and I watch all the shows with animals	122
When was the first time I saw Ella	124
And would it matter if I could sift the truth	125
Helena, your daughter is gone	126
Seven weeks from now	128
Notes	131
Acknowledgments	132

THE PEOPLE

Ella . . . wife of Jake, daughter of Helena, born in Branford, Florida

Jake . . . husband of Ella, newly enlisted Marine assigned to Forty-Nine Palms Marine Base in the Mojave Desert of California

Michael . . . Marine, Ella and Jake's neighbor on base, Ella's lover

Tess . . . Marine wife, neighbor

Tess's husband . . . Marine who sees Ella at the saloon

Caroline . . . Ella's youngest sister

Helena . . . Ella's mother

Grant . . . Jake and Ella's childhood friend

In the pines, in the pines
Where the sun don't ever shine
I would shiver the whole night through

—*Lead Belly*

There is a willow grows aslant the brook

—*Hamlet*

I

Ella

I can smoke a cigarette,
then run a six-minute mile
on a washed-out desert road.

I can make a lemon cake from scratch,
trim and shoe a nervous horse,
feel my way through a pitch black
basement, fry eggs,
scrape the burn
off toast.

Still I wish I'd known about mornings
before I took
your name, moved to the desert.

Mornings in Forty-Nine Palms are like big dumb sunflowers
open as the faces of my blond sisters who bow their heads to pray
even when no one's watching.

Somebody should have warned us.

The breakfast table is a windswept plane
that never disappears at the horizon
because there isn't one—

there's just you,
sitting on a milk crate, eating cereal,
giving me the good chair.

Ella

Prom night in Branford.
Jake tied silver ribbons
to my horse's saddle.

She put her hoof
into his shin.

I could see then from every direction:
Jake cursing and spitting,
surrounded by the swollen sunflowers
of my family's ranch.

And there I was,
a white fleck against
the collage of evening blues—
an ivory button,
an eye tooth.

Ella

I didn't want her.

She'd never worn a bridle, let alone
a saddle. Her teats
dripped on my boots
when I brushed her.

Then I found her twins
dead in the mud.

It had just rained
a hard Florida rain.

Their eyes were sealed shut
with mud, their open mouths
bowls of mud.

And she was just running circles
around their crippled bodies
in the paddock.

I watched my father put the heavy
bodies into black trash bags.

I watched him bridle her and tie her to a fence post
where she stomped and struck the ground.

More blood came out.

I didn't want her.

I named her Red.

Ella

Infinity stretches out between us
and he asks if I'm going to the ranch today.
He nuzzles in my sore tits. I want to kick him
in the shin. Would he tie ribbons
to my saddle, feed me carrot nibs,
bat away the flies?

Jake will always look like a boy
to me, even when he's eighty, his ears are long,
and I am dead.

I have to remind myself
that he's the one in the Corps, not me.

I am the one training to be a window stuck open,
single paned, spider-cracked. No one will be able to close me.

I'll let everything in.

Wind, centipedes, rain, thieves,
the little gnats
that cluster in banana peels—all will come
and go through me and I will feel everything.

Ella

Heart at rest,
muscles cold, fleck of cream
on my chin, I will keep pace
with your right tire for a quarter mile,
you will smile at our game,
I will bite the air,
and after your car disappears in dust
I'll go back,
and you will know all day
that I'm at home
sitting on my haunches,
mouth slightly open,
ears alert
as starting guns.

Ella

Blue kettle knocking
over flames, two cups chipped
in different places,
flies lapping butter.

I squeeze a honey bear
into your black tea,
add a tablespoon of cream.

You are always
about to leave.

In the early-early, you screamed
into the reeds of Parris Island.
The reeds grew sharper, they popped
the nails from your fingers
while the drill instructor,
the one with yellow eyes, lit himself
on fire. And when I woke you,
I wished I hadn't woke you.

Ella

There used to be

a Mojave River that flowed from Soda Lake
to Victorville. There's still a river

but it slunk underground. Hardly anyone knows.
My mother asks me over the phone where'd my love

for Jake go? Who did it?

*Remember how he couldn't dance
that night, Ella? How he sat in a folding chair*

*with an ice pack, watching you, all night
his eyes never left?*

She goes on and on like this, as if it's her marriage
and not mine, as though it's her traveling

under bedrock in a blue current, toes pointed,
arms crossed. *He danced with you,*

even though he didn't dance with you.

Where'd the love go?

It grew perfect gills and scales
and gave itself to the river.

Stop talking and listen for the torrent.
People think something's gone

just cause they can't hear it.

Jake

A fly landed on her shoulder
at the party. She was wearing
nearly nothing and I knew we'd
have six children. She drank too much
Nyquil. She mixed it with Vodka.
I held her hair. I sprayed perfume.
I never told. The fly drank her
sweat because she was so alive.
The river asked us for our sin, Amen,
and I knew we'd have six children.

Jake

At the concert, lighters waved like
thumbs of fire on a placid lake,
smokeless, clean, not a second death
but a tablet of slate to test
the metal we are made of. Gold,
that night our hearts were golden bowls
set floating on the lake of fire.
Ella's lighter kept going out
so I gave her mine, hoisted her higher,
her thighs crowned my head. Soft thorns.

Jake

Ella's first horse, Red, kicked me hard
in the shin. She was jealous or
else she didn't like silver ribbons.
No way she knew what I had done,
only God knew and saw my sin
in the sunflowers tall as me,
lost I was among them, a sheep
in the midst of wolves, a bee caught
in a bed of silky yellow stalks so
soft, slender, nude, bending, quiet.

Grant

They both wore white as if it was their own private wedding and not prom night in the high school gym. Neither of them danced with anybody else, and they danced slow, even to the pop songs, as if they had their own band playing. Ella liked old music, her momma's music—Patsy Cline, Peggy Lee, Loretta Lynn. And Jake just liked whatever Ella liked, which is the best way to be close to Ella. Like what she likes, dance slow—and if she all of a sudden wants to lift Good Bars and Maker's Mark, you better be ready with the getaway car.

Ella

Night played taps with our spines
and the mothers occupied with their scrubbing
ignored us for casserole dishes
and our siblings' cries for cake.

Day is done, gone the sun
from the lakes, from the hills,
from the sky—

I was breaking you for the first time.
Not all the way, just far enough.
I said, Imagine God sees us through the keyhole
and it's not my father, not your father,

not anyone's at all. When it was over,
you picked up the trumpet again
but your fingers refused to play.

I'll press the keys, I said, you just make
the sound. When it's time to walk,
I'll lead you straight past the mothers in their nightgowns,

straight past the fathers playing cards,
the babies in their pens, the dogs at their chains,
I'll lead you into the sunflowers and break you again.

Jake

Will you go with me if I go?
That's what I asked Ella that night
at the springs. Our goal was always
to unblock the mouth of the cave
so we could swim inside. Will you
go with me if I go? One rock
for each held breath but she had gills
and fought like old Leviathan
in the blue wings of algae, the beam
of her headlamp like God's good eye.

Midnight, we hung our slimy legs
over the ledge of slick limestone,
both smelling like dogs halfway dry
and rust and bread. I asked again.
To the desert? she echoed, my
bride, and I was scared she would jump
so I lied on top of her like
I never had but always dreamed except
in the dreams there was light coming in waves,
scents of grass, long stalks, yellow leaves.

And she said let me break you, break
you, break you, break you, break you, break
you, and she put me inside
of her and we walked the desert, broken,
with burning feet and burning hands,
our tongues in one place and our teeth
somewhere else, my veins in her arms,
we became a monster, with our tail
whipped away those spying stars.

Caroline

Momma
spent
weeks sewing.
She burned
at least
five dinners
making it cause
she was
looking
at her hands.
Looking at the needles
in her hands.
Daddy
said stop
burning up the food,
Helena.
Helena is our mother's name.
Like the volcano.
Like the saint.

II

Jake

When I see rabbits, I see him,
chewing, ducking, hiding in grass.
Blame the rabbit for eluding
the child; desire for forgiveness
is the reason I forgive. If
I lie still as a fence post,
so still I become what the wind
doesn't notice, memory will
pass me and move on to the next still corpse.

The recruiter said I could play
trumpet in the Band, sure, the brass
sections always struggled. Drummers—
everybody wanted to hit
things with sticks. He was pale as rice
and had a cleft lip that my eyes
wandered inside and bounced around
in as he told me where he was
the day the towers fell, a dark school gym,
lit by TVs on carts, same place

I was, just in another state,
first week of senior year, zero
hour. The recruiter had a wife,
a preschool teacher with fire red
hair but no freckles, a runner,
running off the baby pounds, ha,
she loved the life, the base exchange,
childcare. And when the towers fell
I just knew, he said, I betcha
that's when you knew, too. How could you not
join when those bodies came
jumping out?

Jake

When the sunflowers are quiet
I am full of noise, a garbage
truck screeching and halting,
garbled scripture, reaching my arm
out, shaking metal cans of glass
and diapers and lawn trimmings.
Once, on Parris Island, my ass
caught a bayonet, seven stitches,
fever-mist eddied foxtails, angel oak,
the bald heads of mallard, thickets

of shrub, the rough throats of Fish Crow.
Illness slinking in brackish lagoons
did not distract the men in gray
who spit blades from across the room,
planted thorn-flowers in my legs,
poured toilet water in my mouth.
When the sunflowers are quiet
I want to stand naked without
my skin, no flesh to hide the soul inside,
just bones waving with yellow kings.

Jake

The oaks of Branford, Florida—
I know them all by bark and crown,
know the white oak from burr and swamp
and chestnut. Young leaves, pinkish down
softer than dog ears, the white oak
is frosty until its acorns
feed deer, mice, ducks, larvae of moths.
The gray bark peels itself away
from itself. Hardpan, wrinkled grandfather
born old, ranting in hurricane

wind. Pond cypress, cabbage palm, slash
pine, you are not God's favorites.
We bury our dead under oaks
so that we can find them again
when their moaning calls us from dreams
and down ladders pitched against
our father's clapboard houses, reeds
bending as we glide like sailing
stones. But in the desert, there are no oaks,
no moans, only pinyon, thunder.

Michael

My head under his boot, my teeth
on the curb, tongue tasting the cold salt.
I'd crashed his truck into a dumpster
drunk, walked home without keys.
Or I'd left his toolbox in the rain.
Or dug a hole and never filled it.
Then my mother's chest, wet
and heaving. Her crucifix would jab
my cheek, leave a tiny Christ
in my skin. Sometimes His tiny feet
would press into a zit and it hurt.
Try to move away from her and she'd scream
crazy woman. Then when I was seventeen
he just stopped cause I was too big
for him and he shrunk down to a dog
that I could kick in the ribs if his hackles showed.
Fight over a steak with me, I'll kick
your ass, Old Dog. But I'll tell you something
one day I saw her fixing her hair up
and I knew it wasn't for him. I pinned her to the wall
that bitch, for a long time . . . not too hard
not so hard I'd kill. Her hands gripped
my hands as my hands gripped her throat
and I saw she wasn't wearing her ring.
Then, you know what I did?
I started laughing. Why the fuck, I said
but I was laughing so hard I couldn't finish
in one breath. I kept my grip and her eyes
big as catfish. Mother, I said
why the fuck
did you wait so long?

Michael

I didn't do it but I helped them
so what does that make me?
The deputies wanted to know.
Something like this could keep you
outta the military, boy, you want that?
Nobody ever asked me what I want
so I don't even know. Tell us what them boys
did to the old woman and we'll
forget about the rope you lent.
Lent, like you think I wanted
it back? A smack to the ear.
Too many details, I gave them all
like I was there, like my mind was a camera.
One of them turned away to puke in a drinking fountain
the other rubbed the butt of his gun
and I knew he wanted to press it to my lazy right eye
and pull the trigger. He has an eighty-year-old mother
who lives alone on the mesa, opens the door
to anyone. But I got off. A cop's son. All I did
was know about it before it happened.
And it was my old man's rope.
Lightning before thunder and I can sleep
through both.

Michael

How do you count backwards
from death? Tire iron, wheelbarrow
handcuffs, field of red poppies
too much static on the radio, spilled cups of coffee
small wrists flying around my head
and chest. And before that, three beers
for breakfast, a boring dawn
my wife saying, "Don't come back."

The first time I went to Iraq
she said the same thing.
Seven months passed, I came back
and tied her to the furnace with jumper cables
chopped wood in the backyard for hours
brought in armfuls of creosote
and juniper, made piles at her feet.

Swinging the ax sorta calmed me
each rise of the ax a number away from death
until my steps took me back to my wife
until my hands undid the ties
and I could cry on her chest.

Michael

When you cry like that, all strung out
like a line of sheets in the breeze, a clot of blood
trembling in your palm.

When you dump your plate
into the sink and leave me at the table
holding my scars
like pink salamanders.

When you tell me to fix it, fix it
fix it.

I think of the one day he walked me home
from school.

We saw a white kitten
with its head stuck in a diamond
of the chain link fence around
the baseball field, blood on its paws
and mouth, crying, kicking its hind legs.
I told him I'd run home for
wire cutters, but he wouldn't have it.

He was teaching me how to let
something die its own death
how to not interrupt God's words
midsentence.

But I pleaded like my mother: I cried her fat wet tears
and put my face in her warm doughy hands
which were my hands
until he pinned my body
which was her body
against the wire fence
held me there with one steel arm
until we all went limp.

Michael

I like seeing people's faces through windshields
lilac and sky blue and seasick green, eyes blinking
gray to white to gray. What's on the screen
doesn't matter as much
as the butterflies half-alive on rusted bumpers
silently clapping
the teenage mom nursing
a smoke from the bed
of a Chevy
the day bleeding palely into night
and the stars resisting the blood
until they can't stand it and thirst means more
than privacy.

Only once did somebody ask me
why I come here alone. A shitty corporal
with buck teeth and no manners.

Where's your girl, Sergeant? You leave her at home?

I flashed my pistol and he got his answer.

Here, I am no one anyone knows; here, I am the knower
and I sort you all out like marbles
or keys or screws.

The blue desert planets burst into view
and nobody sees me.

Jake

War games take me away for weeks,
and weeks turn into black branches
into leaves into birds into
pale yellow stars too far to count.
You have to focus on what's here—
not on the wife you left at home,
not her glasses, her runner's calves.
What you have is open sky, wind,
the wilderness, the scorpions that drink
tears from your blistered palms like saints.

Through the nightmare, a barn owl winks
at the camp of sleeping soldiers.

A mild fever in me lets the owl closer.

Michael

She was dancing like something that twists
when it burns. Iron, titanium.
She turned colors. The pole rusted

when she wrapped herself around it.
I was three shots in and just getting started.

The bouncer was heading for her
but I stopped him, said she was my neighbor
and I'd get her home safe.

We went behind the club and played
with matches, lit some steel wool a cook
had thrown out with the garbage, melted the mouth

of a juice jug until we smelled almonds
hallucinated a dry lake bed
studded with burning horses.

Ella

First time I was alone with Michael,
I left my glasses at home.

He was a totem pole carved
from red cedar and mounted

in a shadowy corner of The Adobe Bar.
Hello, neighbor, he said

and I recognized him despite
the raccoon mask over his eyes,

the eagle wings frozen
mid-flight, the white antlers

covered in dust. We went out back
behind the dumpsters

so we could hear each other speak.
A little dust fell like snow

from his velvet skull bones—
I'm not always like this, he said,

usually I'm just one thing.
Then he listed what he's seen burn:

domes, horses, dump trucks,
birds on a fence. Even objects scream,

he said, and we drank whiskey
from a flask until we were half asleep,

leaning into a slow, slow dance.

Ella

Michael buys me bracelets that I can't wear home
and he has to be the one to take them off,
put them on, move them further up
my arm. If they dangle and make a sound,
he'll take them back. We have to keep things quiet
unless we are far away from people.
Mostly we have to find
the silent parts of our bodies and lie down
in them like canoes.
Knees can be silent if bent, silent if they rise from murky
water like roots. My wrists he loves the best.
Morning light though veins, light parade
of riverways, reddish black as Suwannee,
light silvering the reeds.

Michael

The painted quarter horse
knows when she's got a slow child
on her back. The boy looked into her eyes
before I lifted him onto the special
saddle with all the belts
and clicking locks, and she knew it
right then like the boy had come from her
and there was afterbirth on his face.
She knew that flies would always hang
around his lashes like hungry blue jewels
and he'd never want to leave her shadow.

The ranch hands ask the boy questions
like he's gonna say something
but I know better. He just wants to ride
just wants to feel the sun-warmed leather
until there is no feeling, just being
and he becomes animal
and the close-lipped neigh
is the only sound he needs to make.

I take him round the corral ten times
or more. When his daddy wants to split
and shouts to take him down,
it's a small death. The quarter horse
groans—she's held her bowels the entire hour
and will wait until the boy is off and away
and his cries stop echoing
in the canyon.

You might think that he's crying
cause he has to leave the ranch.
But the horse knows and I know
it's cause his daddy secretly wants him dead
but can't kill him, not all at once.

Ella

The auburn Gelding
and the blond Palomino
stand at the gate
like they've been waiting.
It's our first day at the desert ranch
and I pretend there's no one
expecting me to come back,
no yellow porch light
or unlocked door, nothing steaming
on the stove, just the humming
of the fridge, the flypaper buzzing
and twitching,
sink dripping over a milk jug,
and if I bring you home with me
and my keys hit the bare floor
no one will hear but the half-conscious
craneflies.

The horses, waiting,
are a good sign. They aren't afraid
of you and neither am I
even though
your hands are leather
and smack like halter straps
against our necks and thighs.

Tess

It's true I seen them kissing
on the porch,
where my kitchen window faces Ella's door.
Those little wrists
ringed with a dozen bracelets
and there I am rinsing dishes, staring,
and the staring made them change
like one of those ink blots
or like when a toppled rocking chair
is a bent-back creature skulking
in the den at five a.m. until the light
makes it a buffalo, a mountain,
then finally a chair again. Is it the staring
that makes a man into a bear,
a woman into a deer, white tail fanned,
a long kiss into a python
forever swallowing its meal?
I admit to refreshing my lowball glass
more than once, I admit to pressing
myself to the warm oven after he lumbered
away, to letting a pot boil over and not wiping up
the milky water, I admit
to letting dinner burn.

Ella

Michael wants me like a road
for a truck that won't slow.

No breaks, just blinding light bearing down
on me. I have to create myself

at the last possible second
just to keep him alive.

What if I didn't make a road for him . . .
that's the question I ask and it hangs

like a fruit bat from a laundry line.
If I wasn't here

maybe a cop, maybe a pole, maybe
a ditch would stop his wanting.

Tess

Back in Louisiana, I knew a girl who hooked it
from time to time
just by word of mouth—no advertising—and she stayed busy
in a town of a thousand Baptists.

She started young—her twin brother
would whore her out to his friends
when they were in middle school.
I let her cheat off me in math because she looked like the ghost of Eve
and because I knew she'd still fail.

Long hair past her nipples
and leaves in her clothes
from rolling on the ground
and the tiniest jean shorts all ripped
like humanity clawed
to get back inside.

Eve and her twin brother, Jay, who took off his shirt
whenever he could and smelled like almonds
and patchouli.
They both wore sandals
and had dirty feet. They went to my church,
sometimes,
but always sat way in the back,
giggling.

Probably they knew we'd gotten it all wrong—
the story of who was pure
and who wasn't.

Ten years later I see her picture in the paper.
Jay tried to kill her
with a lamp chord around
her tiny neck and all she had was a stapler.

When the ambulance got to her apartment
they were holding each other,
crying, bloody.

There are all kinds of love stories.

Jake

Born early, the blue hour between
dawn and sunrise, mother's gloved hands
rubbing warmth against my cold night,
tubes of air, glass crib. Understand
I wanted full sun, a ripened
nativity, summer solstice,
to be a clay baked tough as hide,
to offer myself as roof, callus
for your wounds. Ella, here's a cigarette . . .
some coffee. Stay awake with me

until blueness comes, dance for me,
O, Potter, turn me back to dust.

Jake

My dreams unfurl, thousand-petal heads
set upon a deep pool
I can't swim through, not until
I lick my chow plate clean, not until
I punch myself in the stomach
hard enough to lose breath and fall
six flights, like Alice in the hole.
It's not the falling that wakes me,
not the sound of a woman's cold toes
grazing a wooden floor against

the sound of a man's heavy stance
and the flex of his arms holding
her up as he dances her, red
lantern haze swinging his shadow—
it's the drill instructor slapping
my bare thigh, brass knuckles gleaming
in moonlight, sunlight, flashlight. Awake,
the swamp cooler's drone. Then, Ella's
hush stops my mind, scent of lotions, blankets,
my own small hands, ovate fingers,

latticework of bone and vine.

Jake

I jump from the platform, a deep
pool catches my weight, but only
for a second, like hitting branch
before ground. At the bottom, boots.
Boots kicking in slowest motion,
uniforms sucking skin, faces
blurred by escaping air. If my
boots knot themselves together while
I crawl, I'll sink to the bottom, no one
will see and wars will still be fought.

But you can't drown the drowned the way
you can't set fire to Seraphim,
or resurrect a man in love.

Caroline

She
never
played
with me
after Jake
moved in.
I saw
her
in the shed.
She
promised
she'd kill
me
in my sleep
so I didn't
sleep.
Then they got
married.
It was a sin.
What they did
in the shed.

Ella

Now I've failed and the failure tastes
like the desert after fire:

hose water on rooftops,
boiled tar, suncups

of melting ash, bouquets
of sage with no virgins left to catch them.

I would like to take apart the tapestry
but I am old enough to know

there is no undoing
a done thing.

Still, I like to imagine
ripping out the threads.

Rip, rip—away the relatives
with their gifts and casserole dishes

and loaves and cakes—
away my handmade dress.

Away goes Red snaking her head
and pawing the ground.

Jake playing his bugle
each note asking Do You Choose Me?

Away goes my mouth
answering I Choose You, I Do.

Rip, Rip.

III

Helena

Here is what I know about Jake:

The boy was ten years old
when he came to Branford
with his father

He left his youth in a Midwest silo
left his photos
snowshoes   mother

He was a milk flower
turning toward the sun

or he was a bare bone
gaining some skin

So poor all his daddy could give him
was chalk

Then she twirled in

       something with a pull-string
       sent spinning

& the chalk wrote
what the chalk wrote
       E + J forever

we found it on the sidewalk
on the steps   we found it
on his face & neck

Helena

Sensitive
too sensitive for a boy

Jake wrote plays

He thought of titles:

String Flower
Hand in My Hand

He alphabetized his music
    Abba to Zappa

He learned to climb rocks

At night he stared at the sky
wrote poems about himself
staring at the sky

Helena

Jake imagined a string of pearls
or milk stones
when he needed to fall asleep
& how they would look
in a perfect box
in his hands
& her hands lifting up her hair
his thumb & finger
on the clasp
not shaking
not snapping like pieces of chalk

Helena

Jake came to live with us
when his daddy reenlisted

In a house of women

his eyes were baby-blue & huge
as milk-moons reflected in compact
mirrors

When the kids were at school
I'd look through his things

In a diary he wrote:
today I am no one

Once   Ella made him a flower crown
placed it on his head

he wore it for an hour

for an hour he imagined himself
as someone

Helena

Jake grew a whole inch taller
after a month of my casseroles
& milk from our cow

just barely could I see his fawn-colored
hair over the sunflower heads

sometimes I wasn't sure what I saw

his hair rising in the breeze
the flash of an elbow mid-run
a blue eye shrouded in leaves

& other parts of him that fought
shadow & bramble

Boys have a secret world
better left alone by mothers

better met with a silent agreement

a blurred vision that comes & goes

Helena

Her impatience burns her
fingertips & the roof of her mouth

I remember Ella
being bitten by fire ants
when she was five
& eating strawberries

She wouldn't hear me when I said
wait till next month

They will taste better

They will be ready

She didn't feel the fire on her bare toes

until her feet were covered
in red & black

She wanted them as they were

small   wild   sour

Helena

She wanted to wear her prom dress
to her wedding

He'll know me in it she said

She wanted to get married in her home

& so we all set to preparations

We spent days   cutting the edges
of thick white paper with special scissors
drying cornflowers   tickseed   violet salvia

When the day came   she held a bouquet
of firewheels & blazing stars

Jake's leg was mostly healed
he played his bugle & the dogs howled

That was a year ago
but still I can see them shoeless

leaning into each other

a record skipping in another room
blazing stars letting loose

Ella

Sometimes people hide in plain sight,
like my mother, Helena, who was a volcano
in seersucker dresses and Goodwill shoes,
making dinner every night by six-thirty, spreading
mayo on white bread by nine, writing
a note to each daughter that ended
with a line from 1 Corinthians 13.

Summer nights in Branford we'd play sardines.
When you find somebody, you crawl inside
the storm drain or the overturned boat and wait.
You weather. You smell each other's sweat

and breath and you stay despite the rat, the spider,
the hurricane coming closer.

Sometimes people hide like they mean
to stay hidden, like they'll win the hiding game
by any means:
hop a train to the next city,
repel down a ravine,
bury themselves alive.

They hide so well they become lost
even to themselves.

They join search parties, carry lanterns,
cry their own names.

Ella

My father's veterinarian office,
the wide scale, biscuits in a jar,
syringes, cotton swabs, cages,
pills for heartworm, pills for seizures.
The slab of concrete where he'd pace
and smoke Dunhills and call us
at home where we'd be peeling glue
off our fingers, imagining our own skin
could be that painless, waiting
for popsicle-stick barns to dry,
waiting for life to catch us by
the collars, carry us in its whirl.
When storms came, the roof stayed on,
the house bent and kneeled
and beat its own back with a branch
to keep us safe. This close to the earth
you can keep reliving fossils of memories.
I wear them now like my mother's
nightgowns, so thin, like woven shadows
of no real color: grayish lilac, faded clay.
I wear them here in the storm cellar,
I wear them for you, I face
the dusty cans of tomatoes and beans
like when I worked in my auntie's store that summer,
saved up money and bought a bike
which I would ride to meet you at the springs.
I remember all of these things,
I face all the labels out so I can read
them and know what is here
in the earth, in the tomb.

Ella

Dance night in the community center,
a renovated barn with a parquet floor
and Christmas lights dangling
from rafters. My parents
never went except the one night
they did.

        Stay in the truck . . .
        one song and we're done . . .

Country music, the old tunes,
sad songs. Music to hang yourself to.

My sisters and I ate the popcorn
we'd been saving for the drive-in.
We drank the pop and counted all the stars.

I waited until I couldn't.

They were off in the corner
bathed in the blue light of the vending machine.
Blue jeans locked at the zippers,
hands stuffed deep into back pockets,
faces sewn together
at the forehead, eyes closed.

Their love was one animal made of two.

My father hummed to Loretta Lynn's
"Singing the Blues"

Well the moon and the stars no longer shine
    the dream is gone I thought was mine

One time my mother caught me dancing naked
in my bedroom without any music playing.

There's nothing left for me to do
    but cry cry cry cry over you . . .

I don't know what bothered her the most.
She gasped and covered her mouth with her hands,
silencing a scream like in a horror movie.

Her arm fat trembled.

I kept dancing, thinking I could make her laugh,
until she threw my radio
out the open window.

Well I never felt more like running away
    but why should I go cause I couldn't stay

The radio wasn't on, Helena.
The radio wasn't on.

Reach out your hand and touch me.
I'm ten years old with a Dixie jazz band
playing inside my head.

Touch me, Helena,
I'm electric. I'm a dewdrop
popping on the hot skillet. I'm your one tear
falling on the iron
as you press white sheets.

You've got me singing the blues
        You've got me singing the blues, ooh

I was so close to my parents as they danced
they could have felt my breath,
but they didn't even lift their gaze.

I knew then that parents played pretends
the way we kids did.

In their fantasy, we were never born—
we were floating out in a blue space

if we were anywhere at all.

Ella

Say my name into a canyon,
and you'll hear only what you heard
before you ever knew me: open space,
crabapples, mason jars
of rain. You might even knock
on my momma's door
and have her open it to a house
I never lived in. She'll smile and ask
if you're lost and would you like
some sweet tea, and you'll leave
wondering what you even came for,
past the horses in the corral
who will not know you because they never did.

Say my name into a canyon
and I promise the sunflowers
we once lied down in
will cease to mean anything
when you dream them.

Michael

My mother is six months dead
but dad is strong as ever. The evil can breathe longer
than the pure in a house on fire.
She went to sleep on ashy clouds
with a cancer in her brain.
He collected life insurance, bought a hot tub
and a bunch of junk cars. Now we take apart
engines on the weekends, sometimes we
put them back together.
He keeps asking when I'm gonna
have a boy of my own and I don't tell him
about the abortions, the miscarriages
the carnage floating out somewhere I can't see.

How I let the snake die cause I couldn't feed it
pinky mice anymore. How the sight of
uncooked chicken makes me gag and I have to drink
a quart of scotch just to keep from pulling
my own tongue out.

How Lisa and me are wrong
for each other, how we bang
our parts together hard and pretend each thrust
is a sign of life.

How little, scared, pinky mice babies
is all we ever make. Food for owls, food for snakes.

I don't tell him how we fuck other people now
so we don't have to make more carnage.

I guess I don't tell him much of anything,
while he tells me everything, but I don't listen
just like old times.

Michael

She wants to know my plans—
where I'm going, what I'll take.
What's waiting. She taps the splintered sill
with a lacquered nail, a breeze drags
the ocean two hundred miles in a headlock
smells like anchors, rotting docks, salt.
I think I'll go to Long Beach, flop
in the sand like a seal, tunnel around
then go out past the breakers
where even ships can't breathe.
My lungs will be large as mainsails.
My mouth will be wider than a faultline.

Mother doesn't like my answer.

I can tell because she fades a little and I can see
the row of mailboxes through her chest
the yellows and blues of junk mail, the red light
of the radio tower blinking between her eyes.

Where should I go then, mother? You tell me.
How close to death can I get—
how close is too close? Not the ocean, she says
you've got to go farther.

She says, I'm going on a trip to the moon . . .
and waits for me to finish.
I'm going on a trip to the moon, I say
and I'm gonna bring climbing shoes
nylon rope, reinforced steel. I'm gonna bring
my hunting rifle, skinning knife
water-proof boots, explosives in a gunny sac.
But I can't please her, she's leaving, she's mad
and disappearing, and through the curve
of her stomach
a weed patch, an empty plastic bag
the moon flees my touch.

Michael

All day I've had the feeling that I don't belong
in my living room. Like some other man
is going to walk through the door
and find me with his wife, who I thought
this whole time
was my wife.

He'll have just gotten
back from Iraq and want to know
what the fuck I'm doing skinning potatoes
with his knife in his kitchen
and maybe my underwear are his
and the yellow stains he made
with his dick.

I'll walk so long I finally get to the houses
where grass grows. The houses
by the big Evangelical church
where the marines who've become new things try to live.

I once knew a forty-year-old marine turned night-club owner
who shot himself in the head
on his own perfect lawn—drought-tolerant
Kentucky Bluegrass.

He had given his wife and two daughters a thousand
in cash to go shopping in San Diego for the weekend.

The morning they were due to come back,
he cleaned the house to a shine. He put a casket
on layaway at Costco. He even
smoked a brisket, baked cornbread
so they'd have dinner when they got home.
The cops were called exactly 60 seconds
before he pulled the trigger so his body
would be found right away.
The blood didn't even have time to stain the grass.

Michael

At the Break-n-Run Billiards
gray moths crack their carpals
at the ceiling
like little wrists.

I tell myself that tonight I am no one anybody knows.

Just wind over an empty planet.

I introduce myself to the bartender
with just a nod,
then rest my face on the cool wet bar.

I dream I dream I dream of burning horses.

I would have liked to put Saddam inside his own zoo. A cage about half the size
of his shoe closet.

A closet just for shoes. Fuck.

Throw some dried up hay down on the cage floor. Here's some dead moths
for your water bucket. If we feed you it means we're gonna
eat you. If we starve you it means the slowest death you've ever had.

The water has algae growing in it, too.

Almost every time I dream
it's not about the men or women or children . . .

the horses they were on fire

they were looking for water.

. . .

No one like you gets better. That's what my wife said
or maybe that's what the bartender said
or maybe that's what my mother says
in her eternal sleep.

But Ella thinks I'm . . .

    She thinks you're a hero, huh?

    So when she gets in your truck, let her.

    Let her smile at you—

    let her mean it. It's not your fault
    she's dumb as a puppy.

    It's not your fault
    she loves you.

Everything's my fault. I know what I've done. I know I lent the rope.

Pick your face up.   The bartender is real.   Solid as an oak.   Yep. Skin like an oak.

Get your face off my bar.

I dream I dream I dream.

One Halloween Lisa and me went as bears wearing tuxedos and we won some prize.

Now every day is Halloween
as the moths hoard the light and the room goes dark.

She married me. Joke's on her but she doesn't laugh no more.

He's a marine, give him some respect, somebody says about a drunk man slumped on the bar.

I went to war not knowing who to miss and the feeling never went away but it slept and slept and that was good enough.

Helena

With the moving truck carried away by a brown cloud
down Dixon Road   Ella behind the wheel

I set to washing her off

off the door handles & off the floor
& off of me

scrubbing my fingers & behind my ears
under my heavy breasts
scrubbing & soaping
in the porcelain tub I once birthed
a son in

    If Paul had seen that blue face

    To carry inside you something dead
    to know but not know
    to carry on with special vitamins
    & headphones stretched over the belly
    country music played for an empty hall

    If he'd seen the face was his face
    whereas all the girls have mine

& Oh how I've been holding it all in
squeezing my thighs together hard
to keep it all in

my love my anger my sopping wet ghosts

He says I'm haunted
& he might be right
but it's not a ghost that clings to my pant leg
or puts a bone around my neck

This is not to say that I don't love Ella

Lord knows I've suffered for her
Lord knows I'd do it again
Lord knows I will regret washing her prints off the fridge
& soon I'll be hunting for the arches & whorls
of her thumbs
for a strand of her fine fine hair
so fine you'd have to be her mother to know
it is a strand of hair at all
& not a line of spider's silk

Grant

People don't know this, but I married Ella and Jake before they actually got married at the wedding. Up in my fort in the swamp. Their priest and their witness, I made up my own rituals. Pricked each of their thumbs and made them smear their blood together. Jake was worried it was all sin. He was always worried about sinning. But he wanted to screw more than anything so we talked about how hell might not be that bad. Maybe not worse than August in Branford. I had to help Mr. Payne, Ella's father, do a root canal on an old pit bull later that day and I was just smiling the whole time. *What you smiling about, Grant? You in love?* Mr. Payne asked me, his hands deep in the mouth of the pit. *Me? Nah. Well, sorta. Kinda. I'm part of love, I guess.*

IV

Ella

I come to the pool by myself.

Face down in water, I see
heaven from above, angels dividing
like cells, stretching wide
then splitting apart, wing from spindle,
until there are millions
in a watery mesh, and the angels
don't look like people.

Beneath me:
horses, cornflowers, gristmills,
lotus ponds,

dried seed pods
ridding themselves of burden.

Sometimes I see the springs
of Branford, other times I see what's real:
pennies, leaves, a child's sandal.

When I pack up my things to leave,
the marine wives whisper my name
as if I'm already lying in a wooden box
packed with sage,
as if heaven is not a reflection
of everything we've lost.

Ella

An hour late. I stare at Michael's apartment door
from my kitchen window, wrapping
sandwiches in paper.

The wind the wind
is no one's friend.

Oleanders scrape the stucco with their antlers.
Blossoms let go and line the gutters.
My cigarette makes a city of ash
in the tray.

The wind is picking up my tulip pots
one by one and sailing them
across the highway.

Ella

A dove has made a nest under the concrete
awning of our apartment.
She argues with herself
about choosing the right sticks.
This morning I felt the walls,
eyes closed, pretending to be blind,
and found my way around. Then
I jammed foam plugs
way down deep into my ear canals
and tried again. Still I felt
the vibrations of the phone
ringing on the wall. I could live alone
even without sight or hearing,
I could tunnel through the caverns
of the earth and not miss
the radio, the crinkling
of gift wrap, the humming of the fridge.
This place might as well be
a tunnel—then I could close
my eyes for good and spend
my life feeling with my hands,
knowing with my touch.

Ella

Dear Jake,

I will never send this letter.
This letter has a match under it
and whimpers.

Yesterday was your birthday
and I left the phone off the hook.

I ate my nails down to the flesh
and tasted my flesh
and it was vinegar.

You've been deployed just three weeks.

At the pool this morning, a toddler
fell into the deep end
while the mother slept on a lounger.

I was on the shallow side, just getting in
and slow with vodka. I thought
maybe I was deaf because the kid

made no sound. But then a car backfired on the highway
and crows flapped wild from that diseased pine
you said would fall.

When you left in the early morning
while I slept,
you left like this.

Ella

No coyote stops me in the road,
wanting to know my plans.

Nobody at the gas station
will give me a light,

not even the cowboys
who almost always do.

Even the breeze won't touch my neck.
This morning, a lizard carcass

fell from the sky, choosing me.

Tess

My baby I love more than my husband,
but I love my baby as much as I love
my lover, the way he frowns when a little milk
flows into his sucking kiss. My husband
I love more than my father,

who once shaved my head for loving
Darren, a black boy, in the field
behind the barn.

If I could, like a dog, save all my love for just one thing . . .

Not a baby, not a man. Something steel
and gray and shaped like a train
or a long-necked bottle
for me to stare at or
throw across this stretch of tumbleweeds
and crows
like a faithful boomerang.

Ella

In the saloon, a man recognizes me
as Jake's wife. The marine ball, he says,
we met. You spilled a drink
on your man's dress shoes. Maybe
you're a klutz, he says. He has a face
like a bullsnake with scars
around his lips like his mouth
was once sewn shut. We're actually neighbors,
he says. We're all neighbors, I say,
and go out back to the blood orange
moon. After I met Jake
I forgot how to pray because
I didn't need to anymore. Praying
is just giving yourself advice
you will never take. When the blood moon
drips, you must find an alley
and wait. If a bullsnake man
is drunk and wants to fuck you,
if you wait and no one comes,
if your mother's hands appear
in the blood moon, if any of these
or none of these, if a tidal wave
comes towering down the street,
if you see God crouching
near the dumpster, if He winks
and says, Ha-ha.

Tess's Husband

I drink a whiskey sour, but burned brisket
is a hard taste to wash away.
My wife was crying over it,
broom in my hand, punching
the smoke alarm.
Am I dissatisfied? I've eaten fire,
another blackened dinner
means nothing to me.
And there she is at the jukebox, my neighbor,
with her swimmer's tan, her button nose
that's never been broken.
Part of me says she's a shot glass
I'd like to pull from, slam against
the counter. Part of me says
she's not pretty and what's pretty
got to do with it.

Ella

At the carnival, I see Michael
tossing ping pong balls into empty
fish bowls on a picnic table.

When he turns and sees me,
he's got a goldfish in a plastic bag
half-filled with water.

He's already pretty much dying,
Michael says, and then, My wife's here—
on the Ferris wheel.

I turn and leave.

He says something muted,
something about us,
but I'm buying a ticket for the Jump & Smile,

climbing into some kind of carapace,
something discarded for its heft
and darkness, its facelessness

and obsidian sharpness. What did he say?
Something muted. Something about us.
A drive. A new way of being
together.

Ella

Michael wasn't at the meeting place—fooled again.
In my twirling skirt and hiking boots,
I had nothing to do but smoke,
wait, watch the turkey vultures
swim the sky above Coyote Hole.

Because hate doesn't interrupt lust,
it just repeats what lust says
from a barstool in the shadows,

I choose a warm boulder to straddle,
I lick the salt from its rough, Monzonite skin.

I would dive down,
all the way down, I would uncover
every blocked cave
in the circuit of caves. All paths
would be clear, all courses open, every vein
flowing. I would kiss and kiss
and follow the dark stretch
until it ends.

Why won't the earth
open up for me? Why won't it let me in?

Ella

Today I slept for hours on the speckled face
of a coffin-shaped boulder, as vultures
suspended like creaking barrels above me.
I dreamed we held an outdoor ceremony
and no one came.

The empty white pews, covered in frost,
caught leaves and acorns
lost by the one-armed oak
as we stood side by side
in front of a doorless church.

We must have been a couple.
It must have been a wedding.
We must have meant something
to each other.

We looked for gifts under the oak
but found only the linty, bone-filled
hunks discarded by owls,
and so I picked through them
with the quick fingers of a seamstress.
Jaws, beaks, rows of teeth, every
white object that ever was.
Gravestones, fences, crosses, children's hands
making church and steeple.

We looked for cake
but found only a pile of forks licked clean.
The people must have come and gone
and we were the ones who showed up late.

When I woke, the dream kept going.
In the car driving home, the dream kept going.
In the shower, washing between my legs,
the dream never quit. I tried slapping
myself hard as Helena would if she could.
I put a rock in my shoe and walked to the mailbox.
I wrapped your dirty undershirt around my neck
and pulled upwards 'til I gagged,
while those empty white pews, wherever they are, glistened.

Ella

I could go back to the apartment
and answer the phone next time
it rings and I could say, Hello,
Hello, Jake. Hello. Yes, I'm still listening
for the turn of your key.
Yes, I know it's been six weeks.

I could go to the pool at Lucky Park.
I could go to the bar.

I could go back even further,
to my mother,
drive for three days
and set both feet on her porch,
knock with both fists.
Hello mother. Hello father.
Hello sisters.
My name is Ella Payne.
I used to live here
and that palomino over there
in the stable, the lunatic,
her name is tattooed
on my right shoulder
and I've come back to claim her.

Ella

If I go home to Helena,
she will start with my mouth, working
the bar between my teeth, under my tongue,
she will pave my gums, suds
will cascade over my jaws.
Then, she'll have me iron
and fold a dozen bleached white sheets.
She'll sit me down in an upright chair,
splay her dry fingers across the lap
of her apron. She'll open her mouth to tell me
what she thinks of my choices
and something will be in there—a dove?
A clutch of eggs? Seven angels
with trumpets?

I don't know. I can't see. What is it, Helena?
If you think I'm rotten,
you've never been wrong.

Ella

In the absence of my other
I am propelled into open spaces.

I pick a path and then a road
with a sign that is more bullet holes
than sign.

A wind on the horizon sweeps
white sand into its mouth,
spits it out as waves.

When I call them, the men I have loved
come to the corners of my mind,
behind each of my eyes, like shy horses
catching the scent of oats.

Love, you were supposed to be just one man,
one man out of all the others,
knowable as my own hand,
and that was supposed to be enough.

Ella

If I name each place the meeting place,
then I'll never be wrong.

When you arrive, I'll be washing your plate
for the millionth time,

barefoot in a kitchen of sandstone.
My thighs will be crosshatched with scars

and I'll be out of honey. You'll want
to know where I've been,

and I'll say, here, darling. Here.

Jake

A nineteen-hour flight, concussed.
Discharged honorably—only
two months in the shit and old Jake
has to quit. Deaf in the left ear,
"And do you hear a loud ringing
in the right?" the doc asked. No,
I hear crickets, waves, laser guns,
toilets flushing, engines purring,
I hear my father's shoplight zapping moths
and Helena's iron hissing
as it presses damp cloth. I hear

my own sounds and no longer need
others. I am a radio,
I play footsteps, rain on metal,
church bells clanging, bird nests breaking
and crows, hundreds of them, flapping
under heavy nets. A flight attendant
asks something, bends closer, haloed
in static. She speaks in dishes
shattering on hardwood, then backs
away, scared, sweeping as she goes.

Jake

I waited at the terminal
for hours, then tried to get drunk
but couldn't even get started.
Twenty ain't no twenty-one. Shit,
I wish I could give you a drink—
damn shame. The bartender asked me
about my head, gave me a Coke,
on the house. The lights hurt my eyes,
I could not drink what was given to me
but went to the men's room instead

to cry on the toilet and say her name,
head in my own hands,
head like a hive. Five days ago
I was a soldier. Five fingers,
five days. And now, and now. What now?
Ella, I had to hitch a ride
from a stranger. She didn't question why
I rode with my jacket over

my head the whole way, she just drove.
She walked me to our front door, carried
my bags. I couldn't even say
what she looks like. She said the worst
was behind me, but she was wrong.
Ella, I am home. I am feeling
my way from room to room, waiting,
sometimes sitting on the milk crate
feeling for spilled honey on the table,
feeling and finding what you've left.

Ella

Every road is a gamble,
each toss spreads my fate on the table
for the dealer to decide.
How lost did I get myself this time?

You can't measure loss in degrees.

If I could see myself from a low-flying
plane, then I would know.
If I could see from above as when I swim
the surface of the pool.

If I could get up, out—

>Get up out of yourself,
>Helena told me once.

I was making daisy chains
and drinking from my daddy's flask in the basement,
Patsy Cline on the record player,
"Three Cigarettes in an Ashtray,"
skipping and crackling.
She stood in the shadows, not leaving
the last step of the wooden basement stairs.
I pretended not to hear.
Jake was on Parris Island with a fever,
and when he came back
we'd pack the truck and leave for the desert.

The album turned over. Helena
sang along as she climbed the stairs,
leaving me where she found me,
closing the door behind her.

I thought I heard the deadbolt
slide into place. She could have lit
a match and been done with me,
but she went back to her needlework,
still singing here and there,

she was letting me know the walls of her house
weren't really walls,
but doors, and she was
the keeper of the keys. She jangled
her pockets.

Now, I feel my own keys in my hand.

Just a year ago, I would have said God
will lead me to safety. God will wander me
in a circle back to my truck.

Now I say nothing.

If the sky breaks, I'll open my mouth
and cup my hands.

Even my skin will drink.
The swords of the Yucca will catch
plenty. The sky will crack
any time now.

Maybe the trick is to not want.

God is mysterious, God is fickle.

We can't know His ways, said Helena when the wind lifted white tablecloths
from the rented tables
and sent bouquets of baby's breath spinning through the air.

It's not gonna hold, she said, her brown eyes searching the horizon
and watering from the wind.

I stared past her to the barn and the sunflowers.

A few drops is all I need now. I will drink from the swords.

And there was Caroline,
who had been keeping to herself
all morning, rearranging the flowers in the vases on the tables,
standing on a chair to reach,

and the sky cracked open
just long enough to turn the driveway to a river of mud.

She went slipping face first.

Caroline who was born at home. Caroline who still sucked her fingers
at night and was afraid of me.

She's gonna kill me! She's gonna KILL me!
I saw what she did in the shed!

Hushed conversation. I stayed downstairs in my father's study,
a bride alone with her ghosts. I could strip off this dress
and run, I thought.

Caroline in the bath, spilling her guts.

Then I hoped the rain would stay, the rain should flood
the ranch. We'd have to postpone, we'd have to reconsider.

I could strip it all off—
Jake, our plans, the cake in the fridge,
the way he sucks my nipples hard
like he's starving.

I am not a spring eternal.

I will drink from the swords if I can find them, if I can just
get up and out and see from above.

In the shed, the man who was fixing the roof with daddy.
Ella and the man together.
She's gonna KILL me.

Some chairs were moved to the big covered porch.
Forty-seven people packed in. Only the elderly
and pregnant sat. No aisle.

Mr. and Mrs. Jacob O'Brien,
said the preacher.

My name became Jacob. The name "Ella" carried up the stairs
and dropped into the dust.

Jacob and Jacob kissed for everyone to see.

The rain paused.

We snuck away to the back of the house
and took pulls of whiskey
and laughed.
Hello Jacob, Jake said.
Hello Jacob, I said.

And we shared the cigarette I pulled
from between my breasts before
going back to the party
we never wanted.

We danced on the porch.

Fireworks crackled from a mile away.

Danced so slowly
what would anyone watching have thought?

Sometime after dark, grandfather
clutched his heart
in the kitchen while washing up dishes.

We didn't know.

We were sleepy with whiskey
and leaned into each other hard.

We leaned in and I forgot
about the rain. I forgot about Caroline.
The man in the shed.

I forgot about Red, who was unhappy,
and my mother who was unhappy,
and my father who didn't seem to feel
anything at all.

There was a moment where I was
asleep, I'm sure, and my body
was dancing itself without my brain
telling it to.

Some bodies go on like that. The brain
is dreaming and the body dances
itself to a faraway desert.

The body dances itself until it's good
and lost.

Good and lost and passing the same bramble
with the little white sacs of seeds. Bag Lady Bush
is what people call it.

Same stack of jagged rocks I made the last time I came this way.

The bobby pin I dropped. My own bootprint.

If I could just get up, out, like Helena said.

Helena.

She picked me up from my first day of high school.
Everyone else walked or rode the bus or hitched rides
from seniors.

She had pink curlers in her hair. My cheeks went hot.

Go home, Helena.

Don't call me Helena, call me ma or mom or mother.

The heavy door of the Ford truck swung open.

I'll walk, I said.

You will not, she said.

I will never call you anything but your name again, I said.

You are the coldest child I've ever met, she said. When you open your mouth . . .

When you open your mouth . . .

I can't remember the rest.
I go on walking after midnight, out in the moonlight . . . something, something, something . . .
under starlight . . . I'm always walking . . . after midnight . . .

A truck door swings open.

I will call you Mother if you just give me some water.

I try to say it.

My eyes won't stay open.

I am pulled inside.

I'm not going to fall asleep. I am just going to close my eyes.

Maybe just one eye
at a time.

First left, then right. My eyes will take turns, but one will always . . .

The truck might be moving or just idling.

The dark desert is both still and blurred.

Like war. That's what Jake's daddy told us once. Still and blurred at the same time like a watercolor painting, he said.

Watercolor didn't seem so bad.

Helena, Mother, water . . . water, water, water . . .

Tell me something about your day, she said. I want to know what you did in class.

We're not leaving this curb until you talk.

The truck idled in front of my high school
until I was sick from the exhaust, but still I wouldn't talk.

A few hard slaps and then the truck pulled onto the road.

I will drink from the swords. I will call you Mother. If my mouth would just open.

If my mouth would make the sounds.

The truck is going now. The truck rattles and clangs and carries a full load.

One eye and then the other. Still and blurred.

The smell of gas station coffee.
The smell of the cold, empty bowl of desert.
The smell of metal, tools, animals.

I was wrong before. I will say Mother. For water I will say Mother. Mother, Mother, Mother, water, water, water, Mother . . .

What you sayin', girl?

The driver is a man.

Mother, Mother, water, water . . .

One eye, then the other. Blue light. It's just before dawn now. The stars melt on God's tongue. The animals come out one by one. Animals with snowy antlers and parts that rattle and wings of every size and no two the same.

Snowflakes . . . every time your mouth opens . . . snowflakes . . . that's what Mother said.

Michael

My wife asks me about our neighbor,
You know the one, she says. A cop
came by earlier, asking questions.

I'm going to be a cop soon, I tell her.

She's knitting booties for something
that will never have feet.

Missing, she says. Ella.

Water boils on the stove.

I imagine how good it would feel
to throw the pot just above her head.

What did you say? She stops knitting.

But I don't remember saying anything.

If I don't get a badge soon, my tongue
is going to have to come out.
If I can't ratchet my shotgun in a minimart.
If I can't kick a door in.

My dick or my tongue. One of them
will have to go.

Jake

I've come to a wall where the phone
used to be, and dial the air
with a blistered finger. A person
missed is different than a person
missing and one night is one night
and not more than that. Maybe she
got a job watching children
and the parents didn't come home
until late and she is waking right now
and I should make the coffee strong,

warm the milk the way she likes it.
No ghosts yet, no ghosts here
not while I am awake, lucid
in this kitchen where sliced bread still
exists and eggs sit in cartons
not yet expired. Still good, Ella,
you used to check the dates and say
still good. Two months is not so long, Ella.
A record played twice. A joke

repeated. Not a blink, no, but
a long stare at worst. The coffee
is done with its drip and the milk
is boiled, the honey already
sticking to my hands, the table.
My feet, there they go, rising
from the floor.

Jake

The walls pop and shift, expand—moan
with infection. Every cupboard
and drawer is speaking through sewn-up
lips, telling me where her hands were,
what her arms reached for, but not where
she's hiding. When the doorbell rang,
it rung for hours, though nobody
was there, a gift of green label
scotch-whiskey gleaming gold in morning sun.
Someone knows. Someone is watching.

Michael

My neighbor came home.
I saw an old lady take him to his door
like he was a little kid
who got lost and pissed himself.
The lady helped him inside and I heard
the water pipes start up.

Maybe she gave him a bath, maybe
she washed his clothes,
maybe he pretended
he had a mother or a wife
or a friend

until the door closed and silence
came back again.

I tell my wife to go over there
and help him, help the baby,
help the little baby
if she wants a baby so much—

my neighbor with his small hands.
How did he hold his rifle?
How did he hold her in place
for as long as he did?
He was built for a flute,
though I've heard him play the trumpet
late into the night
sobering my dreams, calling me to judgment,
so loud I could taste the
metal inside my teeth.

But now the silence
and the touch. He's touching
his head wrap, amazed, dumbfounded as a baby
in a motorized swing.

The flypaper in his kitchen hangs gray and heavy
with a thousand broken bodies
finally gone still.

Helena

When the call comes
it will be at noon   sweet noontime
taking bread from the box &

delivering it from its clear bag
smudged with the fingers of Caroline
who loves to pick raspberries from the patch
& smash them onto bread

& Paul will arrive with a pound of sliced ham
he bought from the butcher
on his way home from the office

& on this day he'll have picked up
sweets for the girls & picked a rose
from the neighbor's yard

the old record player will decide to work
only skipping twice

when the call comes
it will be easy for me to imagine you as gone
because I could never imagine you anywhere

A desert is just sand

& white space

When I tried to imagine you eating cereal
your scabbed-up elbows on the table the way you did at home

there was no table
no apartment

When the call comes
it will be a bucket of ice dropped into a warm bath

the fleeting feeling of joy
like how I used to feel after making love

wonderful & then
quickly
cold & empty

It will be so like you   my girl
to ruin a moment

& then as though the moment were not enough
all the moments
from all of the sweet noons
that I would ever have

Helena

The white doctor gave me white pills
white as little baby teeth

I kept two from each of you
in an orange prescription bottle
wrapped in a handkerchief

I bet you didn't know that

Really now Ella let me tell you something

I am a frequent visitor of the springs you thought were yours alone

only my spot is secluded
the limestone walls are taller   slicker

The black doctor gave me a mixture   a potion
honey   sulfur   Jimson

You know Jimson because it is the plant I've always said not to touch

Devil's snare   pricklyburr   hell's bells   moonflower

I thought it would be just once

but even my own small world feels heavy

My own small world is a coat closet
& I wear all the coats

Heavy & hot & heavy

So many times I would emerge from the woods
bramble-haired
down to my slip   covered in sweat
pupils wide
looking like a nocturnal moth

& no one but Caroline even knew I'd gone
to begin with

Are you not shocked yet?

I have more

If you call me   if you pick up your phone hanging in the white space
if you press the numbers

I will listen to whatever secret has made you wander off

I have more

When I am at the springs & feeling fine
I see the Suwannee   the Deep Water   the Echo River
going & going from me to you

it knows how to get to the desert
to the white space you have curled into

& all I have to do is let go of the rock face & sink down
down & the current will take me right to you

I have more

I have a currency of secrets

I will exchange blow for blow
tooth for tooth

I will even give you ten for one

Give me just the tip of your finger my Wild One
& I will sharpen the splitting maul myself

Tell me your one secret that has made you disappear
I will give you my neck & draw a bright red X

Right here my Gone One
Bring down your ax
right here

Michael

After I tossed my last twenty
onto the round, red table
the psychic asks me
if I'd mind eating a breath mint.
No offense, she says, and her laughter
was a rusted spring-hinge on a screen door.

She keeps mints close by, she says
for marines like me who come
wandering in with beer breath.
I could have sworn I came here
with friends, at least three, all drunk
like me, but the psychic and I are alone
under a single bulb
in a small, red room.

I eat two mints.
Her lips are not too old
but they're caked in red.
Everything is caked in red.

She shows me some cards

and I see a man and woman
falling from a crumbling tower

a yellow angel pouring water between
two cups

I see myself about to step
off a cliff with a smile.

I think she touched my hands.
One of us leaves the room to smoke
comes back smelling like a campfire
put out with sand and water.

I ask, "Where should I go?"
and we both stare into my hands
until the psychic says I should be getting
home because my mother
is worried, always worried.

Michael

When I was a kid they wouldn't leave
me alone with the class guinea pig—
now they're giving me a dog.

I saw her picture. A black lab
with sad eyes and a blue vest.
Already got a name.

Ginger.

Best if you don't change the name
they said, but I'm going to call her Gin.

She's supposed to lick my face
or nuzzle me when I have my dreams.
Supposed to put her head in my lap when I am strapped to the couch
and can't move.

When I see a dark shape watching me from the doorway.

When there's a sound that doesn't make sense.

When there's blood on the backs of my hands.

Michael

At the Wal-Mart in Forty-Nine Palms,
I let Gin pick out her own chow bowl.

Gin's a service dog, so she can go wherever
the fuck I go. Nobody says a word
though sometimes they look like they want to.

She likes to chew antlers and sticks the best
and she pisses on anthills like I did as a kid
and eats her food fast and doesn't waste
and doesn't beg or bitch or cry.

Quiet. My life is quiet. But not the quiet that comes before
an explosion—it's the quiet that comes after,
once everyone is dead.

I pay the chubby woman at the register
and hoist the greasy, 30lb bag of kibble over my shoulder.

You gotta good dog there, Sir
and I don't know why but I tell her to keep the change
like she's a goddamn waitress.

I say, Let's get out of here, Gin
let's go home
and she knows we share the same home
and she's glad
and I feel the quiet again
and we drive the truck fast
on the highway that is ours alone.

Michael

Lisa's been gone for a week
or maybe a month.

People like you don't change, she said.

But she's not here to see. The house is clean
the windows are open
the kitchen floor is scrubbed
polished as a plate.

Gin and I like to eat dinner off the kitchen floor
sometimes. Like dogs.

We eat steak.

It feels good to be a dog. And sometimes we are bears
and other times lions.

We know this world needs cleaning
we watch what the people do.

People like you.

Lisa, you don't know. You don't see. I change all the time, girl.
Every day I'm something new.

Michael

Gin and I watch all the shows with animals
in them. We bark and growl
when we see starved dogs
left to rot in cages by their owners.

We take drives when we can't sleep.
She knows about Lisa, Ella, my mother . . .
all the women I've made disappear.

Sometimes we see them walking along
one road or another
but we don't slow down.
We don't want to know.

There was one episode where a man died
in his home of a heart attack. He lived alone
with his dog. The dog eventually ate him.

I give you my full permission, Gin, to eat
the best parts of me.

Get the belly first, while it's hot. Eat my fatty liver
and drink my blood. The blood
my angry father and sad mother put into me.
Suck the marrow from my antlers.

If it's winter, wear my pelt.

It won't be easy. The ghosts will come looking for me.

But tell them, woman to woman, that I wasn't so bad
that you knew me better than anyone
and I did love them, but it felt like they were eating me
slowly, and without my permission
eating me alive.

Michael

When was the first time I saw Ella?
Jake wants to know. He's at my door
leaning in like a sick dog, expecting
rice and water from my hands.
I imagine shooting him from a howitzer
and going back to bed. What do I say?
First time I seen her was in a nightmare . . .
her face kept appearing in steel mirrors,
puddles of engine oil, her lips split through
the backs of my hands. When I woke up
she was a moth on my pillow, my bed sheets
were eaten up, and my wife wanted to know
what happened. Lisa was bleeding
from below; she'd lost our third
and I knew it was cause of something
I'd done or was about to do. The apartment
shivered in its own quiet foreshock
as a layer of dust fell like Bisquick
from the ceiling. But this isn't what Jake's
after. He wants to hear me say "covet"
and "thy neighbor's wife." He wants me
to get to the part that's "real life"
as if nightmares aren't real for the both of us
as if he ain't secretly panicking
he's back on Parris Island with a bayonet
up his ass, wondering if I'm the one
who stuck it there or if I'm the nurse
who's gonna pull it out.

Tess

And would it matter if I could sift the truth
from the rye? This is my best dress
and I wear it when I sweep
the bees and oleander buds from the breezeway.
I wear it when I'm on my knees cleaning up
the egg yolk, the syrup, the spilled coffee.
I take it off before my husband comes home
because this dress is just for me—
and now you all have seen me in it.

I'm tired of your questions, I'm tired
of my window facing my neighbor's door
and seeing mourners with their casseroles
and lilies.

Truth is born in circles and dies before it can
be held, like a baby too pure for this world.
You all want to know what happened, but you have to wait until
the next stone gets dropped. And when the future
becomes the now, you'll be back here,
on my porch, asking what happened again,
trying to pick the flame and turnip moths
from the shifting grain.

Jake

Helena, your daughter is gone.
I don't know what it means to be
gone. I feel she is somewhere close
but behind a scrim. Either that
or she's in front of the curtain
seeing everything that ever
was and the whole world is hidden
behind. I fell asleep waiting
for the police to arrive with their guns
and notepads and forms and I dreamed
I was burying her alive.
She was smiling. And when I woke
she was an oak leaning over
me where I lie on the floor
which was soft pampas grass, cool dirt,
no stones. I had to wake two more
times for her to really be gone,
then that heavy knock on the door,
the empty bottle of whiskey spinning
on the floor like the game

where you win and lose by kissing.
Do you own a truck? one cop asked.
Yes, we all do. —Who's we?—Marines,
I said. All my neighbors and me,
we own trucks.—You been
drinking, Corporal?—We've all been,
I said. They stayed a long, long time,
even while I slept and cried and dug dirt
with my hands, searching first for her mouth, her
nose, as the cops drank my coffee,
watched me struggle, squeezed the honey

bear by its head, getting out the last
drops. His head bandage needs changing . . .
it smells . . . open the door, will you?
My head was squeezed and drips honey,
my body sticks to everything
and takes it all home—twigs, deaths, ash,
debris. Look at how he claws the carpet,
I hear one say. Do we wake him? No, wait,
listen, he'll give himself away.

Michael

Seven weeks from now
I'll be on patrol.

I'll be in a cruiser, instead of on foot.
Gin will ride shotgun. My only partner.

This morning, we're out walking by fast food joints and markets
and sleeping drunks.

Forty-Nine Palms, you are my city.
You've been waiting for me to finally say it, I know.
Sometimes I'm slow to the bugle's plea.

I can already hear the calls from dispatch
on my scanner. I can see the radio
glowing red and green. I can feel the weight
of my vest, the points of my star.

The people begin to see me.

I smile at babies and women,
nod to the cowboys, the good ol' boys
the old men with their pocket knives
and paper cups of coffee.

I can hear my father's voice coming
over the static of a two-way radio.
Always have peroxide in your cruiser and in your
cabinets. Make sure your wife is ready.
Blood sets quick, warm water locks it in—
cold water, ice cold is best.

Make sure she knows how to press
without too much starch and get that crease
right down the middle of each pant leg.

But polish your own boots, son. Two hours
a week and your feet will look like volcanic glass.
Start with a horsehair brush to get the grime off
follow with a base coat, polish coat, then shine
with a soft cloth. Your boots tell people
you pay attention, you watch like a hawk
you pluck and clean your meal
before you eat it.

He doesn't know there is no wife to get the crease
just right. No wife to run the tap
'til the water turns cold.

My name is Officer.

My name is Sheriff.

My name is Sir Yes Sir.

My father says he could sense a crime before it happened.
In his bones, he says.
Kind of a pain, kind of an itch.

I'm starting to feel it, red hot in my shoulder blades.

NOTES

Branford is a small town in Suwannee County, Florida, located on the banks of the Suwannee River. This is where Ella and Jake grew up and where they were married just after high school.

Parris Island is a training facility for enlisted Marines living east of the Mississippi River. It is located in Port Royal, South Carolina.

All of the characters in this book are based on compilations of both real and imagined people. The events and the town of Forty-Nine Palms are also compilations.

ACKNOWLEDGMENTS

2River Review: "My baby I love more than my husband," "And what if I could sift the truth from the rye"

Bateau: "The white doctor gave me white pills"

Blue Fifth Review: "A fly landed on her shoulder," "At the concert," "Ella's horse kicked me in the shin"

Diagram: "Prom night in Branford"

Juked: "Michael wants me like a road," "Michael buys me bracelets that I can't wear home"

Poet's Billow : "I didn't want her" (winner of the Bermuda Triangle Prize)

Poet's Billow: "Night plays taps with our spines," "Will you go with me if I go?" "The oaks of Branford, Florida," "Infinity stretches out between us," "In the saloon, a man recognizes me," "Born early, the blue hour between" (winner of the Pangaea Prize)

Red Paint Hill: "I come to the pool by myself"

Sonora Review: "My father's veterinarian office"

Waxwing: "It's true I seen them kissing," "She was dancing like something that twists"

For their time and thoughtfulness, my sincere gratitude goes out to: Jennifer K. Sweeney, Kristin Bock, Jonathan Maule, James Cushing, Roxane Beth Johnson, Joseph Millar, Karen Kevorkian, Gail Wronsky, Chuck Rosenthal, and all of the editors at What Books Press. Thank you, Gronk, for lending your art for this cover. Thank you to everyone who will read this book in front of an audience and breathe these characters to life again and again. Additional adoration and gratitude to Ox from Rat, and to Bear from Bug. Big thanks to my mom—patron saint and earth angel—and to Dave for teaching me how to ask "why," and to my dad for reading to me every night when I was a child.

L.I. HENLEY was born and raised in the Mojave Desert town of Joshua Tree, California. She is the author of two chapbooks, *Desert with a Cabin View*, and *The Finding*. Her second full-length collection, *Starshine Road*, won the 2017 Perugia Press Prize. She is the recipient of The Academy of American Poets University Award, The Duckabush Prize in Poetry chosen by Lia Purpura, and two prizes through The Poet's Billow. Her work has appeared in *Glass*, *Rhino*, *Hayden's Ferry Review*, *Rust + Moth*, *River Styx*, *Diagram*, *Waxwing*, *Phoebe*, and *Entropy*. With her husband, poet and percussionist Jonathan Maule, she edits the literary and visual art journal, *Aperçus*. Visit her at www.lihenley.com.

LOS ANGELES

OTHER TITLES FROM WHAT BOOKS PRESS

ART

Gronk, A Giant Claw
Bilingual, spanish

Chuck Rosenthal, Gail Wronsky & Gronk,
Tomorrow You'll Be One of Us: Sci Fi Poems

PROSE

François Camoin, *April, May, and So On*

A.W. DeAnnuntis, *The Mysterious Islands and Other Stories*

Katharine Haake, *The Time of Quarantine*

Mona Houghton, *Frottage & Even As We Speak: Two Novellas*

Rod Val Moore, *Brittle Star*

Chuck Rosenthal, *Coyote O'Donohughe's History of Texas*

NON-FICTION

Chuck Rosenthal, *West of Eden: A Life in 21st Century Los Angeles*

POETRY

Kevin Cantwell, *One of Those Russian Novels*

Ramón García, *Other Countries*

Karen Kevorkian, *Lizard Dream*

Gail Wronsky, *Imperfect Pastorals*

What Books Press books may be ordered from:
SPDBOOKS.ORG | ORDERS@SPDBOOKS.ORG | (800) 869 7553 | AMAZON.COM

WHATBOOKSPRESS.COM

www.ingramcontent.com/pod-product-compliance
Lightning Source LLC
Chambersburg PA
CBHW020418080526
44584CB00014B/1390